Material Matters

Metals

Carol Baldwin

Chicago, Illinois

Printed and bound in China
10 09 08 07 06
10 9 8 7 6 5 4 3 2 1

Library of Congress Cataloging-in-Publication Data

Cataloging-in-publication data is available at the Library of Congress

Baldwin, Carol, 1943-.
  Metals / Carol Baldwin.
    p. cm. -- (Material matters)
  Includes bibliographical references and index.
  ISBN 1-4109-1672-3 (library binding-hardcover) -- ISBN 1-4109-
1679-0 (pbk.)
  1. Metals--Juvenile literature. I. Title. II. Series: Baldwin, Carol,
1943- Material matters.
  QD171.B24 2005
  546.3--dc22

This leveled text is a version of Freestyle: Material Matters: Metals.

Acknowledgments
Page 4/5, Associated Press; 4, Corbis; 5 top, Corbis; 5 mid, Art
Directors & Trip/H Rogers; 5 bott, Getty Images/ Photodisc; 6,
Science Photo Library/J Amos; 6/7, Corbis/ William Manning; 7,
Corbis/Alain Nogues; 8; 8/9, Corbis/ James A Sugar; 9, Science
Photo Library/A Syred; 10, Art Directors & Trip/A Lambert;
10/11, Corbis/; 11, Gareth Boden; 12, Getty Images/Photodisc;
12/13, Art Directors
& Trip/M Peters; 14, Tudor Photography; 14/15, Powerstock/L
Miller; 15, Corbis/Christine Osborne; 16, Powerstock; 17, Science
Photo Library/Russ Lappa; 19 left, Science Photo Library/Crown
Copyright/ Health & Safety laboratory; 18, Peter Gould; 19 right,
Corbis; 20, Jeff Edwards; 20/21, Corbis/Robert Essel; 21, Science
Photo Library/F.S. Westmorland; 22/23, Corbis/Paul A Souders;
22, Art Directors & Trip/H Rogers; 23, Art Directors & Trip/S
Maxwell; 24/25, Science Photo Library/Chris Bjornberg; 25,
Science Photo Library/C.D. Winters; 26/27, Getty Images/
Photodisc; 26, Science Photo Library/
V Fleming ; 27, Science Photo Library/Oscar Burriel, Latin Stock;
28 right, Science Photo Library/P Goetheluck; 28 left, Art
Directors & Trip/E James; 29, Science Photo Library/Roberto de
Gigieno; 30/31, Corbis/Georgina Bowater; 30, Science Photo
Library/P G Adam, Publication Diffusion; 31, Science Photo
Library/M Bond; 32/33, Science Photo Library/Rosenfeld Images;
32, Corbis/Tom Bean; 33, Science Photo Library/P Ryan; 34/35,
Corbis/ Archivo Iconografico; 34, Art Directors & Trip/G Horner;
35, Getty Images/Photodisc; 36/37, Corbis/Bob Rowan; 36, Trevor
Clifford; 37, Corbis; 38, Art Directors & Trip/
A Lambert; 39 left, Art Directors & Trip/A Lambert; 39 right,
Corbis/David Reed; 40/41, FLPA/B Henry; 40, Art Directors &
Trip/J Ellard; 41, Getty Images/Photodisc; 42/43, Digital Vision/;
42, Science Photo Library/Dr Jeremy Burgess; 43, Science Photo
Library/ Alex Bartell; 44, Science Photo Library/Crown Copyright/
Health & Safety laboratory; 45, Corbis.

Cover photograph of the Guggenheim Museum, Bilbao, Spain
reproduced with permission of Pictures Colour Library

Every effort has been made to contact copyright holders of any
material reproduced in this book. Any omissions will be rectified
in subsequent printings if notice is given to the publishers.

Contents

Any words appearing in the text in bold, **like this**, are explained in the Glossary. You can also look out for some of them in the Word bank at the bottom of each page.

Metals All Around Us

Metals in our lives

Metals can be found in unexpected places:

- in our blood and bones
- in foods and tap water
- in soil and green plants.

Metals are materials that are shiny. You can hammer metals and pull them into wires. Metals allow electricity and heat to pass through them easily.

Metals are vital to our world and our lives. For example, many buildings, cars, trucks, and planes have metal frames.

Wendy Craig Duncan carries the Olympic torch under water. It is on its journey from Athens to the 2000 Olympic Games in Sydney, Australia.

Word bank   metal material that is shiny and lets electricity pass through it easily

Olympic metals

Metals play a very important part in the Olympic Games—the top three athletes in each event get gold, silver, or bronze medals.

Before the games even begin, a special torch is lit in Greece. Then it is carried to the place where the Games are being held. Part of this journey is under water. The flame of the torch is able to burn under water because of the metal magnesium. There are fireworks at the opening and closing ceremonies. They get their brilliant colors from metals.

Find out later...

...how metals are made into sheets.

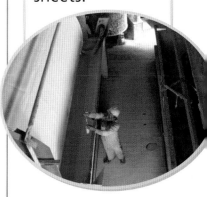

...why metals are used in glassmaking.

...why the Statue of Liberty is green.

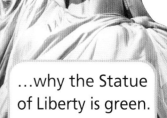

Properties of Metals

Magpies are birds that collect shiny objects, like **metals**, and put them into their nests. Aluminum foil, silver forks, and gold rings are all shiny. This **property,** or feature, of metals is called **luster**. Chromium has a high luster. For a long time, it was used for car bumpers and door handles to make them look shiny and attractive.

Sometimes metals become dull. A dull metal can be cleaned and polished.

Shiny silver

Silver shines very brightly when it is polished. This silver kettle was as shiny as the spoon. But it became dull over time.

Word bank   particle small part of something

Pulling strength

All materials are made up of tiny bits, or **particles**. Metal particles stay close together. Metals cannot be pulled apart easily. They are good at standing up to strain. This property is called **tensile strength**.

Metals are good for making cables. This is because of their high tensile strength. Cables are used for bridges, lifts, and cranes.

Titanium

Titanium is a light and strong metal. Its tensile strength is high and it does not **corrode**. Titanium is used in racing bikes and to replace some human joints.

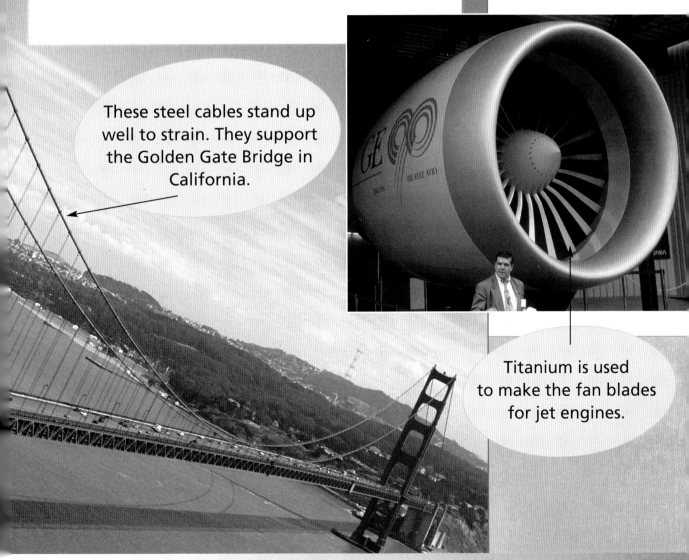

These steel cables stand up well to strain. They support the Golden Gate Bridge in California.

Titanium is used to make the fan blades for jet engines.

corrode **become damaged by chemicals**

Flattened into thin sheets

You can hammer and roll many **metals**. They do not break. This means these metals are **malleable**. Copper, gold, and silver can be hammered into jewelry. This can be done because these are malleable metals. Aluminum is also a very malleable metal. It can be rolled into very thin sheets called **foil**. It is easy for us to fold aluminum foil around a sandwich.

Gold leaf

Gold is the most malleable of all the metals. Gold leaf is made by beating or rolling gold into very thin sheets. Often, the sheets are so thin that you can see light through them.

Gold leaf was used to decorate special books and statues.

Word bank   malleable can be hammered, rolled, or shaped without breaking

Pulled into wires

Many metals are **ductile**. This means you can pull them into long, thin wires. Copper, aluminum, and platinum are some ductile metals. Copper wires are used for electric cables in homes. Most power lines are made from aluminum. This is because aluminum costs less than copper.

To make a wire, a metal is heated and pulled through a hole. Different sized holes make wires of different thicknesses.

Musical wires
This is a **magnified** guitar string. You can see it has a center of metal **strands**. There is a different, thicker type of metal wrapped around the outside.

Aluminum sheets are rolled to make them into foil. Foil is a thousand times thinner than the sheets.

If some metals are
heated in a flame,
they produce
certain colors.

This metal is
potassium. We
know this because
it burns with a
violet flame.

Conducting heat and electricity

Heat or electricity pass through some materials
easily. These materials are called **conductors**. **Metals**
are good conductors. Silver is the best conductor.

Other materials do not let heat or electricity pass
through them. These are called **insulators**. Wood,
rubber, and plastic are good insulators. Electric
wires are covered in plastic or rubber. This stops
electricity passing through people. They do not
get electric shocks.

conductor material that lets heat or electricity pass through easily

Magnetic metals

Magnets are fun to play with and are useful, too. Some metals are magnetic. Iron, nickel, and cobalt are magnetic.

Lodestone is a rock that contains iron. It is a natural magnet. The Ancient Chinese found out three **properties** of lodestone. All magnets have these properties:

- they attract iron
- they always line up in a north-south direction
- you can use them to make other magnets.

Magnetic Earth

Earth acts like a giant magnet. This is because there is **melted** iron and nickel inside Earth.

A compass needle is a magnet. The red end is always pulled toward Earth's North Pole.

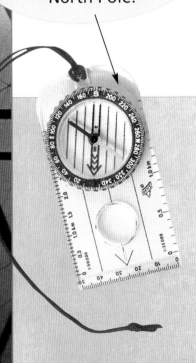

---

insulator material that does not let heat or electricity pass through easily

A bright idea

Tungsten is used to make the **filaments** in light bulbs. This is because it has the highest **melting point** of any metal. When electricity passes through the filament, the heat does not melt it. The filament just glows.

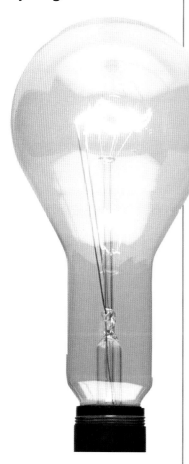

Density

Most of the **metals** we use are very hard. They also have a high **density**. This means that an object made of metal is heavier than the same object made of another material, such as plastic. The density of iron is five times greater than the density of plastic.

Melting points

Most metals have to be very hot before they **melt** and become liquid. But mercury is liquid at room temperature. Room temperature is usually about 68 °F (20 °C). It is the only metal that behaves like this.

Boiling points

Most metals have very high **boiling points**. Iron **boils** at 4,982 °F (2,750 °C). Water is a **non-metal compound**. It boils at 212 °F (100 °C).

Iron melts at a temperature of 2,795 °F (1,535 °C).

Giving off rays

Some metals give off invisible rays or tiny **particles**. This is called **radiation**. Materials that give off radiation are **radioactive**. Uranium is a metal, and it is radioactive.

The rays from radioactive materials damage living things. They can cause cancer.

Danger!
The symbol below warns us that radioactive materials are present.

radiation invisible rays or particles given off by a material

Atoms and Elements

All materials are made from tiny **particles**. They are called **atoms**. An atom has a center part called a **nucleus**. The nucleus has two kinds of even smaller particles. **Protons** are particles with a positive charge. **Neutrons** are particles that have no charge.

Electrons are particles that are outside the nucleus. They have a negative charge. The number of electrons is the same as the number of protons. So the charges balance. Overall, the atom has no charge. It is **neutral**.

How many compounds?

There are thousands of different compounds. The yellow color in this paint comes from a compound. It is called cadmium **sulfide**. It contains the **metal** cadmium and **non-metal** sulfur.

Everything in this photograph contains elements and compounds.

Word bank   compound material made from the atoms of two or more different elements joined together

Elements and compounds

A pure material that is is made up of just one type of atom is called an **element**. Over a hundred different elements have been discovered.

Sometimes different types of element join together. These are called **compounds**. Water is a compound. It is made up of two elements. These are hydrogen and oxygen. So water contains two different types of atoms.

Elements in ancient times

Most elements have always been around. But in ancient times, people used only nine. These were gold, silver, copper, tin, iron, lead, carbon, nickel, and sulfur.

This coffee pot is made from copper. It has become dull over time.

The Periodic Table

Symbols of elements

Every element has a symbol. Symbols are a short way of writing out the element's name. They are mostly one or two letters. The first letter is always a capital.

Scientists arrange all the **elements** in a chart. This is called the **periodic table**. The elements are arranged in order. This depends on the number of **protons** they have. Hydrogen has one proton, helium has two protons, lithium has three, and so on.

This cup is silver. The symbol for silver is Ag. This comes from its **Latin** name *argentum*.

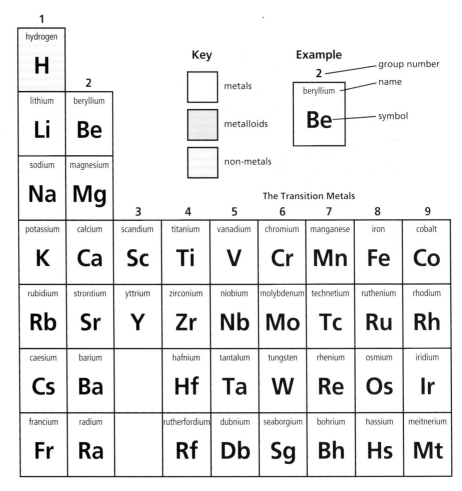

Word bank periodic table chart with elements arranged in groups

Groups of elements

The columns going down the periodic table are called groups. Elements in the same group have similar **properties**. You will also notice a line that goes down the table in steps. This line divides the **metals** from the other elements. All the elements to the left of the line are metals, apart from hydrogen.

Metalloids

The **metalloids** are special elements. They have some properties of metals and some of **non-metals**.

Filling in the gaps

A Russian **chemist** named Dimitri Mendeleev made the first periodic table in 1869. He left gaps to make his table work out. He knew that some elements were still not discovered.

			13	14	15	16	17	18
								helium **He**
			boron **B**	carbon **C**	nitrogen **N**	oxygen **O**	fluorine **F**	neon **Ne**
10	11	12	aluminum **Al**	silicon **Si**	phosphorus **P**	sulfur **S**	chlorine **Cl**	argon **Ar**
nickel **Ni**	copper **Cu**	zinc **Zn**	gallium **Ga**	germanium **Ge**	arsenic **As**	selenium **Se**	bromine **Br**	krypton **Kr**
palladium **Pd**	silver **Ag**	cadmium **Cd**	indium **In**	tin **Sn**	antimony **Sb**	tellurium **Te**	iodine **I**	xenon **Xe**
platinum **Pt**	gold **Au**	mercury **Hg**	thallium **Tl**	lead **Pb**	bismuth **Bi**	polonium **Po**	astatine **At**	radon **Rn**
darmstadtium **Ds**	roentgenium **Rg**	ununbium **Uub**		ununquadium **Uuq**				

This metal is gallium. It was discovered in 1875. It filled a gap in the periodic table.

metalloid element with some properties of both metals and non-metals

17

Groups of Metals

Group 1
Although hydrogen sits at the top of group 1, it is not a metal.

hydrogen
H
lithium
Li
sodium
Na
potassium
K
rubidium
Rb
caesium
Cs
francium
Fr

The **metals** in group 1 are on the left side of the **periodic table**. They are lithium, sodium, potassium, rubidium, caesium, and francium. All these metals are silvery solids. They have low **densities** and **melt** at low temperatures. As you go down the group, the **melting points**, **boiling points**, and hardness of the metals decrease.

The group 1 metals are the most **reactive** metals. In nature, they are always found joined to other **elements** in **compounds**.

The pure sodium metal on the left is stored in oil. This stops it from reacting with oxygen and **water vapor** in the air. This has happened to the piece on the right. That is why it is so dull.

Francium is **radioactive**. It is the only group 1 metal that is.

Word bank   water vapor water in the form of a gas

Uses of group 1 metals

There are many uses for the metals in group 1 and their compounds. Here are some examples:

- lithium **hydroxide** keeps the air clean in spacecraft and submarines
- sodium chloride is common table salt
- potassium hydroxide is used to make soap
- some "electric eyes" that open doors use caesium compounds
- rubidium is used in televisions.

Potassium in your diet
The body needs potassium to keep the heart and **nerves** healthy. Bananas contain lots of potassium.

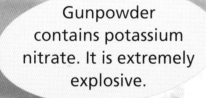

Gunpowder contains potassium nitrate. It is extremely explosive.

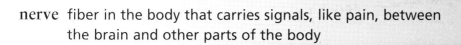

The metals in group 2

The **metals** in group 2 of the **periodic table** are beryllium, magnesium, calcium, strontium, barium, and radium. They are always found in **compounds** in nature, not by themselves.

The group 2 metals are very **reactive**. They easily take part in chemical **reactions**. But they are not as reactive as group 1 metals. They are all gray-white and shiny, but quickly become dull in air.

This symbol tells you that a material can kill.

beryllium	
Be	
magnesium	
Mg	
calcium	
Ca	
strontium	
Sr	
barium	
Ba	
radium	
Ra	

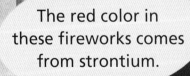

The red color in these fireworks comes from strontium.

Uses of group 2 metals

The **mineral** beryl is a compound of beryllium. Green emeralds are made of beryl. Emeralds are used in jewelry. Magnesium is an important mineral for the body. Plants need it to make food.

Pure magnesium is strong and light. It is mixed with other metals and used to make cars, planes, and spacecraft. Barium sulfate is used in medicines, paper, and fireworks. Radium is **radioactive**. It can be used to treat cancer.

Calcium is everywhere

This snail needs calcium to build its shell. Calcium is in teeth and bones. It helps blood to **clot** when we cut ourselves.

clot thick mixture of semi-solid liquid

Metals in glassmaking

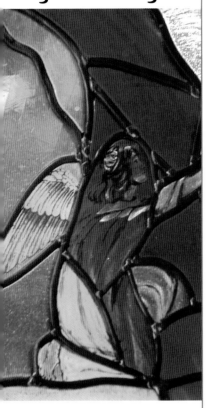

Metals or their **compounds** are added to glass to make beautiful colors. Iron and nickel make glass light green. Glass with cobalt added is deep, bright blue.

Transition metals

Transition **metals** are found between groups 2 and 3 of the **periodic table**. They do not **react** with other materials as easily as the metals in groups 1 and 2 do. They can be pulled into wires, hammered, or rolled. They will not break. They are good **conductors** of heat and electricity. Apart from gold and copper, they all have a silvery shine.

Properties of iron, cobalt, and nickel

Iron, cobalt, and nickel are all magnetic. Their **densities**, **melting points**, and **boiling points** are all nearly the same.

Iron horseshoes and nails were first used about 2,500 years ago.

steel alloy, or mixture of iron with small amounts of other metals added

Uses of iron, cobalt, and nickel

Iron is used to make **magnets**. Strong, permanent magnets have nickel, cobalt, and small amounts of other metals mixed with iron. Most iron is used to make **steel**.

Nickel and cobalt are often found in steel. Nickel is also used for **plating**. This is when a thin layer of nickel is put on top of another metal to protect it.

Rocks from outer space

The center of Earth contains nickel. Nickel is often found in **meteorites**, too. This may mean that meteorites and Earth were formed at about the same time.

The Hoba meteorite is in Namibia. It is the largest ever found. It hit Earth about 80,000 years ago.

Copper, silver, and gold

Copper, silver, and gold are often found as pure **metals** in nature. They do not **react** easily with other materials. All three metals are soft. They can be easily pulled into wires, hammered, and rolled.

For thousands of years, coins and jewelry have been made from copper, silver, and gold. Copper is used in electrical wiring and water pipes. Silver is used to make **flatware**, mirrors, and film for cameras. Gold is useful for coating switches in electronic **devices**.

copper	zinc
Cu	**Zn**
29 64	30 65
silver	cadmium
Ag	**Cd**
47 108	48 112
gold	mercury
Au	**Hg**
79 197	80 201

These six metals are close together in the **periodic table**. But they have different **properties**.

Slang name
Copper was used to make buttons for uniform jackets. Police officers in the United States wore these in the 1800s. This is where the name "cop" comes from.

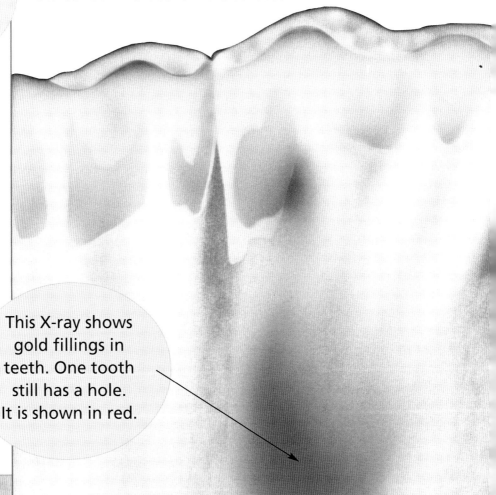

This X-ray shows gold fillings in teeth. One tooth still has a hole. It is shown in red.

device thing made for a special purpose

Zinc, cadmium, and mercury

Zinc is hard and difficult to shape. Cadmium is soft and can be cut with a knife. Mercury is a liquid at room temperature. It has a high **density**.

Iron is often **plated** with zinc. This stops iron from rusting. Zinc is also found in batteries. Cadmium is used to plate metals, too. Nicad batteries contain cadmium. You can recharge Nicad batteries. Light switches and **fluorescent** lamps contain mercury.

Odd one out
Mercury would not become solid even in a freezer. It **melts** at -38 °F (-39 °C). This is a much lower **melting point** than any other metal.

This blob of mercury is very **toxic**. Just touching it can make a person ill.

fluorescent material that gives off light

Aluminum
Aluminum is the most common **metal** in Earth's **crust**. The pure metal is strong, has a low **density**, and is a good **conductor** of electricity. It is used to build airplanes because it is strong and lightweight. Foil wrap and cooking pans are also made from aluminum.

Soft drink cans are aluminum. It is easy to cool these drinks because aluminum is a good conductor of heat.

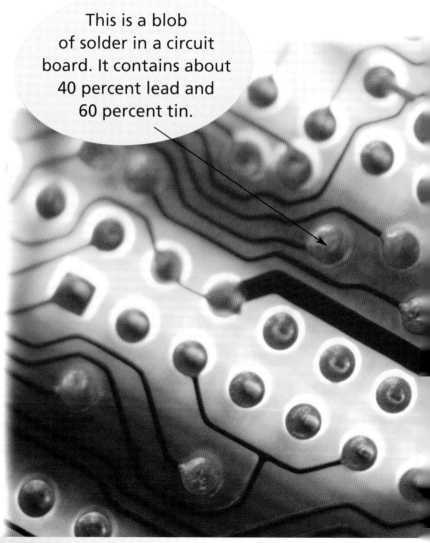

This is a blob of solder in a circuit board. It contains about 40 percent lead and 60 percent tin.

Tiny amounts of iron and titanium make sapphires blue.

Lead

Lead is a dull, gray metal. It is fairly soft and very easy to shape. But lead harms people and the **environment**. Lead is used in car batteries.

There is a lot of lead in **solder**. Solder is used for making electrical connections in television and computer circuit boards.

Lead absorbs **radiation** very well. This is because it has a high density. It is used to protect people and equipment from radiation, such as X-rays.

Dangerous paint

Before 1978, paint had lead in it. When it became old, the paint flaked, and some children put it in their mouths. Some of these children got lead poisoning. This can cause brain and **nerve** damage. Thankfully, today's paints do not contain lead.

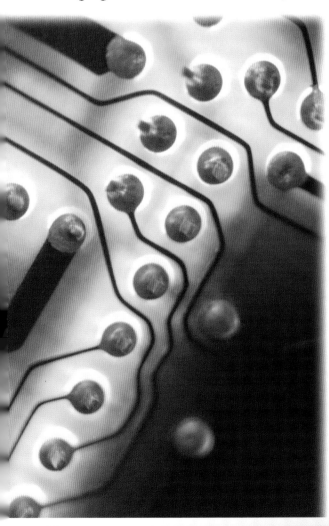

---

solder alloy, or mixture, that is melted and used to join metal parts

From Mines to Manufacturing

Panning for gold

Miners, like the one below, often pan for gold in streams. They swirl water around a mixture of sand, gravel, and gold in a pan. The sand and gravel wash over the sides. The heavier gold dust is left behind.

One of the first **metals** to be used by people was gold. Pure gold is often found in Earth's **crust**. It was probably noticed because of its shine.

Gold and platinum are not **reactive** at all. They do not form **compounds** easily. So pure gold and platinum are found in layers in the ground. These are called **deposits**. Copper and silver are more reactive than gold and platinum. But a few deposits of pure copper and silver have been found, too.

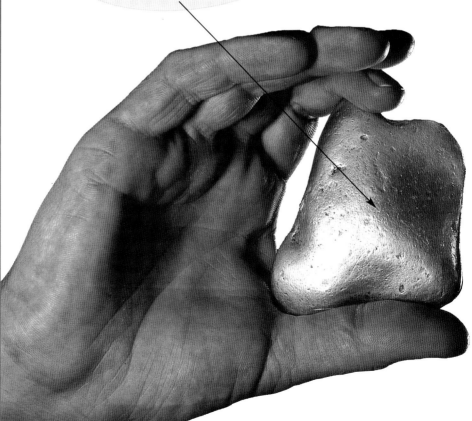

Gold is often found in lumps. These are called nuggets.

Word bank   deposit layer of metal, coal, or other material that is in the ground

Metal ores

Most metals are found as compounds. These compounds are called **ores**. The metal usually is combined with one or more **non-metals** in an ore.

- a metal joined to oxygen is called an **oxide**
- a metal joined to sulfur is called a **sulfide**
- a metal joined to carbon and oxygen is called a **carbonate**.

Metal	Name of ore	Chemical name
aluminum	bauxite	aluminum oxide
copper	chalcocite	copper sulfide
iron	hematite	iron oxide
lead	galena	lead sulfide
mercury	cinnabar	mercury sulfide
zinc	zinc blende	zinc sulfide

Colorful ores
This is a piece of scheelite. It was found in Brazil. Scheelite is an ore of the metal tungsten. It can be many colors.

Mining

Metals or metal **ores** are removed from the ground by mining.

Open-pit mining

Open-pit mining is used to reach very large amounts of ore. Soil and rocks are removed until the miners find the ore. They use huge drills or explosives to blast the rock away. Sometimes a whole mountain is removed. The ore is carried up in trucks or on **conveyor belts**.

Damage from surface mines

- Plants and animals lose their homes
- Soil is washed away
- Flooding

Most of the world's gold is mined in South Africa.

This is a copper mine in Arizona.

conveyor belt endless, moving belt that carries things from one place to another

Opencast mining

In opencast mining, the top layer of Earth's surface is scraped away. It is used to mine ores that are close to the surface and where the rocks are soft.

Shaft mining

In shaft mining, a deep **shaft** is dug downward into the ground. Tunnels are dug in different directions from the shaft. The ore is drilled or blasted into chunks. The chunks are taken out of the mine by mine cars or by **hoists**.

Damage from shaft mining

The water in mine shafts can **react** with **minerals** in the rock to form **acids**. The acids drain into streams and ponds and **pollute** the water.

Iron **oxide** leaked from old coal mines into this canal. Hardly anything can live in the water.

---

pollute put harmful materials into the environment

Getting pure metal from ore

Ores are **compounds**. To get a pure **metal** from an ore, a chemical **reaction** is needed. Chemical reactions often need energy. This energy is usually heat or electricity.

Smelting

Smelting is used to separate metals from **oxide** ores. A metal oxide, like iron oxide, is heated with **coke**. Coke is a type of carbon made from coal. Coke produces carbon monoxide gas when it is heated. The carbon monoxide grabs the oxygen in the ore and the iron is left over.

This is an abandoned copper mine in Alaska.

Roasting

To remove a metal from a **sulfide** or a **carbonate**, you need two steps. **Roasting** is the first step. This is when the ore is heated in air. This produces an oxide. The smelting process is the second step.

Electrolysis

Magnesium and sodium are often found as chloride ores. **Electrolysis** is used to obtain the pure metal from these ores. The ore is **melted**, and a current of electricity is passed through it. This causes the metal to separate from the chloride.

Ore from the ocean
Lumps of metal ores lie on the seabed. They are called **nodules** and are about the size of a fist.

A blast furnace changes iron oxide to iron. This is called **smelting**.

These are manganese nodules.

electrolysis using electricity to separate a metal from an ore that has been melted

Alloys

Many of the **metals** we use are not pure **elements**. They are **alloys**. An alloy is a mixture of a metal and one or more other elements. An alloy has different **properties** than the properties of the elements in it.

How pure?

Pure gold is shiny, but it is soft. Copper is less shiny, but harder. Copper is added to gold to make an alloy. This alloy is harder than pure gold and less easily damaged. It is much more useful for making jewelry than pure gold.

Musical alloys

You will find tubas, trombones, and trumpets in a brass band. Brass is an alloy of copper and zinc.

alloy mixture of a metal and one or more other elements

The first alloy

About 5,000 years ago, people **melted** copper and tin, and mixed them together. This new material was the first alloy. It is called bronze. It is stronger and lasts longer than either copper or tin. Bronze was so widely used that this time in history is called the **Bronze Age**.

Pewter

The Egyptians, Chinese, and Persians made pewter over 2,000 years ago. They made it from tin, copper, and lead. But lead is a **toxic** metal, and this was a problem. Today, pewter has zinc, bismuth, and antimony instead of lead. It is harder and shinier, too.

Not what they say they are

Some Canadian and U.S. coins are called nickels. But they are only 25 percent nickel. They are made from a copper and nickel alloy. In the UK, "silver" coins, like the ten pence piece, are made from a copper-nickel alloy. They are not silver at all!

People stopped using bronze tools, like these arrowheads, when they learned how to **smelt** iron.

Bronze Age period of history from about 3,500 B.C.E. to about 1,000 B.C.E.

35

Steel alloys

Steel is an **alloy** of iron with a small amount of carbon. Some steel contains other **metals,** too.

Nickel steel does not **corrode** easily. So it is used to make gears and cables for machines, such as cars.

Stainless steel has some nickel and chromium in it. Kitchen equipment and medical instruments are made from stainless steel. This is because it is strong and does not corrode easily.

Manganese steel is very hard. It is used in railroad tracks and armor plating for tanks.

Automatic sprinklers are found in offices and schools.

corrode become damaged by chemicals, including oxygen and water in air

SMAs

Shape Memory Alloys (SMAs) are very useful. They can be formed into certain shapes and then bent into new shapes. When they are heated, they will go back to their original shape. SMAs are usually made from nickel and titanium.

SMAs can be used to unblock people's blood vessels. They can also be used in braces to straighten teeth and to join the ends of broken bones.

SMAs in space

The radio **antenna** on the Space Shuttle is made from shape memory alloys. During the launch into space, the antenna was folded up. The SMA warmed up when it got into **orbit**. Then the radio antenna unfolded into its original shape.

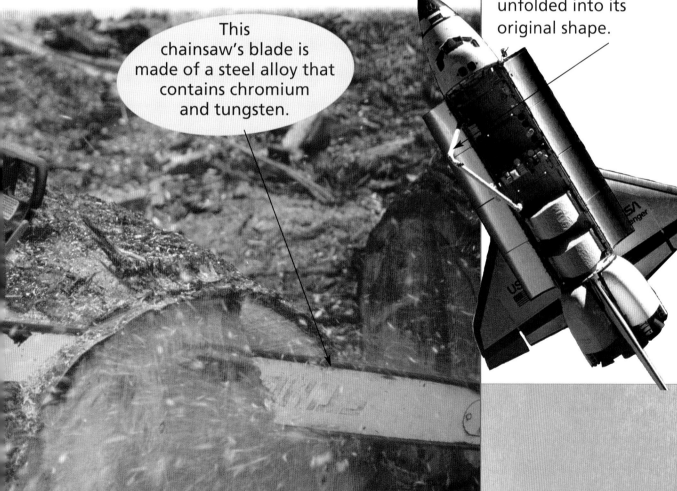

This chainsaw's blade is made of a steel alloy that contains chromium and tungsten.

Metals and Their Reactions

Metals take part in many kinds of chemical **reactions**. When a chemical reaction takes place, new materials are formed. The new materials have different **properties** than the materials they were formed from.

Metals and water

Most metals do not **react** with water. However, the metals in group 1 do. They are very **reactive**. These are lithium, sodium, potassium, rubidium, caesium, and francium. These metals are stored in oil so air cannot reach them. Air contains **water vapor**, and this would react with the metals.

The reactivity series

The metals that are listed above hydrogen in this list will react with acid.

Potassium
Sodium
Lithium
Calcium
Magnesium
Aluminum
Zinc
Iron
Tin
Lead
(Hydrogen)
Copper
Mercury
Silver
Gold
Platinum

more reactive

less reactive

Potassium reacts with water to produce a **hydroxide** compound and hydrogen gas. The gas catches fire because the reaction produces heat.

Word bank   hydroxide compound that contains a metal and an oxygen-hydrogen group

The group 2 metals do not react as violently with water as the group 1 metals. So most do not have to be stored in oil. Magnesium, calcium, strontium, barium, and radium do react with water, however.

Metals and acids

Some metals react with **acids** while others do not. The reactivity series is a list of metals (see left). It shows which metals react with acids. The most reactive metals are at the top. The least reactive metals are at the bottom.

Turning green

People often wear copper bracelets to treat **arthritis**. Some people get a green stain on their skin from the bracelets. This happens because weak acids in sweat react with the copper. A green copper **compound** forms.

This zinc is reacting with hydrochloric acid. Bubbles of hydrogen gas are formed and rise to the surface.

Metals and oxygen

Antoine Lavoisier was a French **chemist**. In 1789, he heated some mercury. He watched the silvery liquid **metal** change into a red powder. He realized that the mercury had combined with the oxygen in the air. A new **compound** was formed. This was called mercury **oxide**.

Most metals will form oxides when they are heated with oxygen. Iron **oxidizes** slowly without being heated. This is called **rust**. **Reactive** metals, like sodium, **react** more quickly in air.

Protecting iron

To stop iron from rusting, it can be **galvanized**. The iron is dipped into **melted** zinc. A thin coat of zinc sticks to the iron. Zinc does not **corrode** in air. So it protects the iron.

Iron reacts faster with oxygen in the air when water is present.

oxidize react with oxygen to form an oxide

Aluminum oxide and iron oxide are used to grind and polish surfaces, like glass lenses.

Metals and other gases

Some metals react with other gases. Copper often has a green coating. The coating is copper **carbonate**. The copper reacts with water and carbon dioxide in the air. Silver does not react with oxygen. But it does react with hydrogen **sulfide** in the air.

Red statue

The Statue of Liberty stands at the entrance to New York Harbor. The statue was made of shiny, red copper. But it now looks dull and green. This is because the copper has reacted with carbon dioxide in the air.

Recycling Metals

It takes a lot of energy to produce pure **metals** from their **ores**. If we **recycle** metals, we can save a lot of energy. Recycling also reduces the need for mining, and it saves **landfill** space.

Ores are **nonrenewable** resources. It takes millions of years to form them. Recycling will make our supply of metals last longer.

Recycling aluminum

- Recycling one aluminum can saves enough energy to run a television for three hours.
- Only 42 percent of aluminum cans are recycled.

Every year, millions of cars end up in scrapyards.

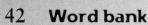

Word bank landfill place where waste and garbage are buried

Recycling iron and steel from cars

Recycling cars is a challenge because cars are made from so many different materials.

Liquids, gases, and parts that can be reused are removed first. The car is crushed and fed into a huge shredder. Giant **magnets** separate the iron and **steel** from non-magnetic metals. The iron and steel are used to make more steel. The less valuable materials are usually burned or taken to a landfill.

What is in a car?

- More than 1,543 pounds (700 kilograms) of steel
- 396 pounds (180 kilograms) of iron
- 154 pounds (70 kilograms) of aluminum
- 44 pounds (20 kilograms) of copper

There are many materials in this scrapyard. This giant magnet is picking up only the iron and steel.

nonrenewable cannot be replaced once used up

Find Out More

American Chemical Society

The American Chemical Society has a division especially for school students. This provides teacher and student resources, competitions, a magazine, and a Web site.

Contact them at the following address:
American Chemical Society, 1155 Sixteenth Street, NW Washington, D.C., 20036

Books

Blashfield, Jean. *Sparks of Life: Iron and the Trace Elements*. Chicago: Raintree, 2002.

Riley, Peter. *Straightforward Science: Materials and Processes*. New York: Franklin Watts, 1998.

Snedden, Robert. *Smart Science: Materials*. Chicago: Heinemann Library, 1999.

World Wide Web

To find out more about metals, you can search the Internet. Use keywords like these:

- "Bronze Age"
- metals +alloys
- metals +recycling water
- elements +"periodic table"

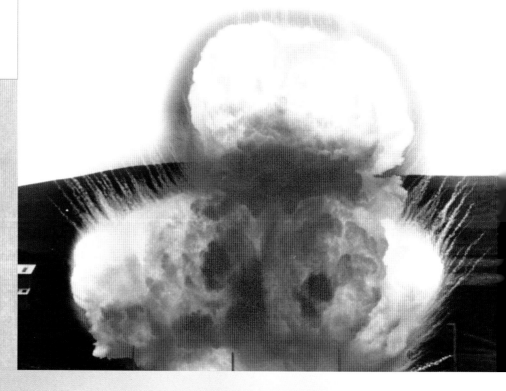

You can find your own keywords by using words from this book. The search tips below will help you find useful Web sites.

Search tips

There are billions of pages on the Internet. It can be difficult to find exactly what you are looking for. These tips will help you find useful Web sites more quickly:

- know what you want to find out about
- use simple keywords
- use two to six keywords in a search
- only use names of people, places or things
- put double quote marks around words that go together, for example "shape memory alloy"

Where to search

Search engine
A search engine looks through millions of Web site pages. It lists all the sites that match the words in the search box. You will find the best matches are at the top of the list, on the first page.

Search directory
A person instead of a computer has sorted a search directory. You can search by keyword or subject and browse through the different sites. It is like looking through books on a library shelf.

Glossary

acid compound that has a sour taste and can burn

alloy mixture of a metal and one or more other elements

antenna radio or television aerial

arthritis painful, swollen joints

atom tiny particle that makes up everything

boil rapid change from a liquid into a gas

boiling point temperature at which a material changes from a liquid to a gas

Bronze Age period of history from about 3,500 B.C.E. to about 1,000 B.C.E.

carbonate compound of carbon, oxygen, and another chemical element

chemist scientist who studies chemical reactions

clot thick mixture of semi-solid liquid

coke form of carbon made from coal

compound material made from the atoms of two or more different elements joined together

conductor material that lets heat or electricity pass through easily

conveyor belt endless, moving belt that carries things from one place to another

corrode become damaged by chemicals

crust outer layer of Earth. We live on Earth's crust.

crystal solid with particles laid out in a regular, repeated pattern

density amount of mass in a certain volume of something

deposit layer of metal, coal, or other material that is in the ground

device thing made for a special purpose

ductile can be pulled into a wire

electrolysis using electricity to separate a metal from an ore that has been melted

electron tiny particle outside the nucleus of an atom with a negative charge

element material made from only one type of atom

environment surroundings of a living thing

filament thin wire in a light bulb

flatware knives, forks, and spoons

fluorescent material that gives off light

foil very thin sheet of metal

galvanized covered with a thin coating of zinc to prevent rusting

hoist equipment for lifting up heavy loads

hydroxide compound that contains a metal and an oxygen-hydrogen group

insulator material that does not let heat or electricity pass through easily

landfill place where waste and garbage are buried

Latin language of the ancient Romans

luster shine that metals have

magnet object that attracts iron and steel

magnified made to look larger

malleable can be hammered, rolled, or shaped without breaking

melt change from a solid into a liquid

melting point temperature at which a material changes from a solid to a liquid

metal material that is shiny and lets electricity pass through it easily

metalloid element with some properties of both metals and non-metals

meteorite chunk of rock and metal from outer space that has crashed on to a planet

mineral nonliving solid material from Earth

nerve fiber in the body that carries signals, like pain, between the brain and other parts of the body

neutral with no electric charge, neither positive nor negative

neutron particle in the nucleus of an atom with no charge

nodule small, rounded lump

nonmetal material that has the opposite properties to metals. Nonmetals break easily, are dull, and do not conduct heat or electricity well.

nonrenewable cannot be replaced once used up

nucleus dense, positively-charged center of an atom

orbit journey, or path, around a large body in space, like Earth

ore metal combined with other elements

oxide compound formed between an element and oxygen

oxidize react with oxygen to form an oxide

particle small part of something

periodic table chart with elements arranged in groups

plating covering with a thin layer of metal

pollute put harmful materials into the environment

property feature of something

proton particle in the nucleus with a positive charge

radiation invisible rays or particles given off by a material

radioactive materials that give off radiation

react change chemically and produce new materials

reaction chemical change that produces new materials

reactive easily takes part in chemical reactions

recycle treat in order to use again

roasting heating an ore in air to produce an oxide

rust iron oxide

shaft vertical hole in the ground

shape memory alloy alloy that returns to its original shape when heated

smelt separate a metal from its ore using heat

solder alloy, or mixture, that is melted and used to join metal parts

steel alloy, or mixture, of iron with small amounts of other metals added

strand very thin wire

sulfide compound of sulfur and another element

tensile strength ability to stand up to strain

toxic poisonous

water vapor water in the form of a gas

Index